FOREWORD

Family law and the l [illegible] a long way since the Cleveland [illegible] ulnerable circumstances still [illegible] would wish to protect them [illegible], relatives, lawyers and all of those who work within the remit of the Family Courts. Putting children first is a worthy aspiration, yet day after day we see cases where the system has failed to deliver on this promise.

Living as your Hero is one person's guide to helping people who suffered abuse as children without receiving any protection at the time, and who are now living with the consequences. The message is a simple and loving one. Be the person you truly are and then decide whether or not to seek redress for past misdeeds.

Shereen Lincoln writes from personal experience of the extent to which the legal system can help. Equally she is honest about its limits. She argues forcibly for inner self development to overcome the traumas of an abused childhood as much as for the prosecution of those responsible, often decades later.

This is both a guide and a reflection. It will be invaluable to all those who seek a better understanding of what childhood abuse means, and how we deal with its traumatic effects.

As Sub-Treasurer of an Inn of Court I know this will extend to all the Lawyers and Judges who work in this field.

Patrick Maddams FRIBA
Honorary Society of The Inner Temple - July 2012

CONTENTS

"What a Hero!' we say when someone sees danger and successfully guides people to safety. In this booklet the same name is given to people who strive against the physical and psychological harm of childhood sexual abuse by learning to protect themselves from its effects.

From my own and others experience with this far reaching crime, there is much heartache about how unfair it was for an adult to steal our childhood. Finding peace and moving on is often a much longer journey than pursuing a court case.

Fortunately we do not have to wait for justice to be served by someone else before we can balance and improve our lives; each time we act responsibly, remember to uphold emotional rights and strengthen our support networks we create a more rewarding, safe and humane way to live.

Positive change can start when sexual abuse stops... reporting it gives everyone opportunities for better.

A POSITIVE IMAGE OF YOU

Our subconscious mind is powerful as it takes what we believe, whether positive or negative, and moves us in that direction. Make this work in your favour!

Take a few moments to create a picture of yourself that is fulfilled and as you do, imprint it deeper into your mind by listening to a favourite piece of music and/ or releasing your favourite scent.

Take a few deep breaths then imagine ...You...living happy and content... Where is it? What is around you? Is anyone with you? What objects, colours, sounds, smells come to mind? Picture it happening now at the age you are?

From time to time, review this exercise and be open to change; as your experience grows your ideas and needs can change.

Make a start! Draw and or write your answers below titled 'My fulfilled self!' You can always expand to a bigger piece of paper later if you like.

DAILY ROUTINE

Abuse denied your right to choose what happened to your body and your life. Recovery reclaims it. Make it your daily business to say, hear, think, focus in ways where you **invest in the best way to see yourself**.

This could be through your reading, therapy, spiritual practice, personal development, writing or art. There are so many admired people from around the world who turned their lives around by doing exactly that. Join them! Daily effort leads to bigger results!

PERSONAL EXPERIENCE

Twice a day, morning and evening I affirm the power of my life to create anew. Each time I decide to invest in more loving, empowered attitudes about myself, the more energetic I feel - bigger and stronger than the low regard I was treated with.

Sometimes the effort makes only 1% difference in that moment to outweigh my negativity or sorrow but I can see and feel how greater strength, confidence and peace have grown within me through doing so and how I don't react to situations in the same way any more.

OVERVIEW ABUSE

WHO ARE ABUSED?

1 in 6 young adults said they had been sexually abused before they had reached 16. 33% said the crime happened more than once and 60% said it happened after violence in their family. The most common age group to experience this crime is 5 years to 14 years.

WHO ARE ABUSERS?

8 out of 10 children know their abusers; e.g. family members, friends, neighbours babysitters; some hold positions of trust, many are even in relationships with another adult. They are all skilled in building then breaking trust.

WHAT IS ABUSE?

Child sexual abuse includes touching and non-touching behaviour.

Touching abuse

- Touching a child's private parts, or genitals
- Put things inside the mouth, anus or private parts of a child
- Forcing a child to touch someone sexually
- Forcing a child to have sex with either with an adult or other children

Non touching abuse

Encouraging children to:-

- watch pornography,
- look at adults genitals,
- be photographed in sexual poses,
- undress or use the bathroom.

Other forms of abuse and neglect

- Somebody knows about abuse but fails to take action to stop it.
- Tricks or threatens others to keep a secret
- Involving others to hurt someone

EFFECTS OF ABUSE

Difficulty to express painful emotions and change unwanted behaviours which can lead to:

- Self harm or mutilation
- Sexual and relationship problems
- Abuse of drugs and alcohol
- Involvement in crime
- Depression
- Eating disorders
- Suicidal tendencies
- Antisocial behaviour
- Lack of anger management

OTHER EFFECTS MAY LEAD TO:

Flashbacks and nightmares

You may find memories of the abuse will suddenly appear, be it during the day or in recurring nightmares

Shame and guilt

You may blame yourself for the events; suffer from low self-worth or feel too embarrassed to get help.

Intense anger

Often directed at the abuser this emotion may appear out of nowhere, especially if you haven't seen them for a while. (You may have feelings of wishing to confront them or completely ignore and avoid them). The anger may feel more general.

Difficulty with intimacy

You may find that you form very intense intimate relationships or even that you avoid them altogether.

Lists of sexual offences after 1st May 2004 - **www.legislation.gov.uk/ukpga/2003/42/contents**

or before May 2004 **www.legislation.gov.uk/ukpga/Eliz2/4-5/69/contents**

Difficulty to take care of self, even hating own body

Scared of becoming an abuser; of being rejected for speaking truth or accused of lying.

Alone
You may feel completely alienated and isolated by the events of your past and expect them to stay that way.

Feel dirty, ruined, without hope

Untrusting of adults, especially if someone appears too familiar.

Healthy sexual relationships involve Consent, Respect, Consideration, Willingness to hear feelings

CARE, PREPARE & PLAN 1
LOOKING AFTER FEELINGS

ANGER

Deep anger for the way you were treated in childhood is understandable. Finding healthy constructive ways to vent these feelings is essential for your wellbeing.

Tick the actions that could help you channel anger and answer the question:

Actions	Tick	Who or what do you need to do them?
Write a diary		
Exercise		
Paint		
Attend a self development workshop		
Support a group that is making positive efforts about a world issue		
Talk, with a close friend or a counsellor (Sometimes strangers are easier to talk to. Look on the Resources page for contacts)		

GRIEVING

It is not unusual to feel sadness and a sense of loss for your stolen childhood. You need to let the feelings out and not be afraid that once you do they won't stop. Learn to welcome these tears; as you allow them out, you should begin to feel more in control.

What makes crying more comfortable? Circle your favourites

A private place

Time with friend or a Counsellor

Watching a sad movie

Wrapping up in duvet

Balm tissues

Hot water bottle

Teddy Bear

COMPLETE THESE SENTENCES

Calming down is easier when:

Hearing the sound of watching/looking at ______________________________

____.

Thinking about ____

____.

Smelling the scent of ____

____.

Tasting ____

____.

Laying on ____

____.

Dancing to ____

____.

Breathing deeply while ______________________________________

____.

Personal Experience

My preferences are to walk in nature, swim, relax in a hot bath with sweet smelling oils, massage and dancing. A little effort in my weekly routine keeps a balance that aids recovery.

PREPARING FOR A LEGAL CASE

LEGAL JUSTICE

We each have a responsibility for our actions towards each other. Inflicting harmful behaviour on each other is not acceptable and the laws are created to punish those who do. Reporting childhood sexual abuse gives opportunities to create positive change and ensure the harmful behaviour stops.

POLICE

Which is the best department to contact?

Contact the local police station nearest to where the crime occurred and officers from the specialist Child Protection Unit (CPU) will speak with you about any past or present childhood sexual abuse. To locate your local station call 101 or click http://www.met.police.uk/local/index.htm

Where can you speak to the police?

In your own home or at the local police station nearest to where the crime occurred.

Who can be with me?

Its ok for someone you trust to stay while you speak to the police; this can be someone you know or an Independent Sexual Violence Advisor (ISVA), based at police stations, Sexual Assault Referral Centres (SARCs) and Rape Crisis. Lists of ISVAs are available through 'rape crisis' and 'the Survivors Trust' websites. Victim Support can also help (see resources)

What happens while I speak to the police?

Questions will be asked to help you give the fullest description of what happened and will be recorded either on paper or tape. This document will be called your witness statement. You will have the chance to check that it is accurate before signing the final printed copy.

How long does it take to complete a statement?

The police know that it is best to go at your pace and not rush the process. It can take a couple of hours, sessions, days or even weeks

What happens once the statement is complete?

The police will investigate your case. If they find enough evidence the police will pass it to the Crown Prosecution Service (CPS) who upholds The Prosecutor Code to ensure criminal trials are in the public interest, likely to result in conviction and prove guilt beyond reasonable doubt.

What's the point of talking to the police when there may not be enough evidence to jail them?

If the police cannot press charges for a criminal case or it doesn't result in a conviction then ALWAYS SEEK SPECIALIST LEGAL ADVICE from a specialist personal injury lawyer about the possibility of starting a civil case which could result in a compensation award. Your courage could also help to bring others to safety; information about child abuse is taken very seriously indeed; it can help to strengthen other victim's cases, protect other children who be around them (safety orders could be issued) or even prevent them from working with children.

The Victims Code sets out the rights of victims, the role of the police & the CPS.

www.victimsupport.org.uk/~/media/Files/Policy%20and%20research/victims-code-of-practice.ashx

CARE, PREPARE & PLAN 2
PUTTING ACROSS THE BEST OF YOURSELF

GENTLE TIME BEFORE MEETINGS

Plan relaxing activities before and after you meet with the police or solicitors; over tiredness can increase moodiness and lack of concentration.

Stay away from people and places that bring conflict or stress as much as you can; giving your statement and thinking about the investigation is more than enough to deal with.

THE MAIN POINTS

When preparing to speak to a solicitor, keep a note of who was involved, where and when things happened, whether any helpful documents or people are available to support your case.
Do you have any questions? Make your list and let the police and / or solicitors know you would like answers

THE PLACE

If you choose to talk to police at home or even if you need to make calls to them or your solicitor think about where and when is the best time to talk to prevent disturbances from others.

DURING MEETINGS

Ask a person you are comfortable with to stay with you while you speak or to meet you there when you leave. Don't forget, understanding each other can take time so its fine to say:

- 'I'm unclear what you are asking/saying - when you said (x) did you mean (y)?' or
- 'Can you ask that question in a different way please?' It's also perfectly ok to say ....
- 'I need a break' or even
- 'Feels too much to continue today'

Positive change can start when sexual abuse stops... reporting it gives everyone opportunities for better.

AFTER MEETINGS

(Remember your Care, Prepare and Plan 1!!!)

- Speak to trusted person /people and let them know how it went.
- Write down, draw, even dance out any thoughts and feelings - expressing them outside reduces the pressure inside!
- Exercise! Deeper relaxation often follows relieving tension!
- Bubble bath? Read inspiration? Watch great film?

ASK YOURSELF ....

Do you need to follow up with any further questions?

Did they:

- ask you about your questions?
- show understanding?
- acknowledge that it is a difficult experience to talk about?
- explain who would be part of the team working on your case?
- were they patient and calm ?
- were you comfortable with them and their expertise?

Personal Experience - police

Most challenging moments:-

Approaching the police for help when my past experiences said not to trust them. Realising that moving on meant I had to describe tearful, painful memories to the police even when I was feeling unprotected and mistrusting.

Reassuring moments

I felt respected, believed and supported, even when my memories were confused. I was often reminded that I was a child at the time of the crime who needed safety, care and protection; abusing adults not children are responsible for the crime. Didn't feel so alone! Felt part of a strong protective team.

Most surprising moments

Realising I had let go of so much guilt! My negative expectations of police gradually dissolved and were replaced by warmth and kindness for the detectives and support staff within the Child Protection Unit.

SOLICITORS

SOLICITORS

They can share their knowledge on the areas of law that have been broken and the types of compensation that may be available to you. Those who care about quality standards, ethical codes and keeping up to date with any relevant legal changes join professional bodies such as The Association of Child Abuse Lawyers - ACAL and Association of Personal Injury Lawyers - APIL.

To find a specialist solicitor feel free to contact them for someone practising in your area. (see Resources for contact details)

FIRST MEETING OR CALL

The first discussion is usually free of charge. The solicitor will need an outline of what happened, who was involved, where and when. It is also your opportunity to ask questions to check who you feel most at ease with. Once you decide on the solicitor, they can also help you to explore various ways to receive funding.

Remember to 'Care, Prepare & Plan'- Put across the best of yourself on pg 18

PAYMENT

- Legal support is a costly business. Fortunately there is help available.
- Paying for yourself - you can negotiate stage of payments with solicitor.
- 'No win, No fee' arrangements (sometimes called conditional fees)- payment is only taken on winning.
- Legal aid (sometimes called public funding) - some or all of the costs can be paid, depending on your income.
- Personal or employment insurance - legal fees for personal injury can be part of your policy.

OBSTACLES TO CLAIMING COMPENSATION FROM...

A) **Individuals** may not have sufficient financial resources to pay so the court may reject the case, particularly if it is filed outside of the usual legal time limits. However you CAN still apply for Criminal Injuries Compensation.

B) **Institutions** can say that

- their employee(s) were acting outside the responsibility of their work or
- professional and care standards at the time were acceptable
- there is not enough relevant document, evidence and witnesses

C) **Time limits and Court's discretion**

While it is common for survivors to need twenty or thirty years before disclosing the crime, the law requires cases to be brought to the court within specific time frames. The court can, and often will make exceptions, particularly in claims against local authorities. Professional legal advice will definitely give you a strong chance to secure it!

HOW IS PERSONAL INJURY PROVED IN A CIVIL CASE?

In the main the evidence needs to show a strong likelihood that psychological harm and/or physical injury was caused to a child through unsafe standards of care and inadequate protection.

A case can be brought against:
an individual (eg/ family member, family friend) or an institution or a company's employee(s) (eg/ workers in a hospital, school, church, childrens home, youth or sports club)

Remember, 'Care, Prepare & Plan' before you call to put across the best of yourself on pg 18

Daily action to respect your own life is always in your control, no matter how long a case may take or what its outcome may be.

Personal experience

Pursuing a case needs an emotional health warning! Its very demanding and often uncomfortable to face challenging legal formalities while sharing past traumas. With all the lengthy letters, forms and waits between each unfamiliar legal stage my anxiety, awkwardness and fear rose, especially when expected to talk with unfamiliar staff about my case.

Finding strong evidence is a difficult task, especially many years after the crime so **it's vital to find** someone who can give **honest assessments in balanced, sensitive and thoughtful ways.**

My first solicitors were not as helpful or as thorough in sharing information as the second and it was the emotional support from Victim Support that helped me cope at such a confusing time.

PATHWAYS TO COMPENSATION IN UK

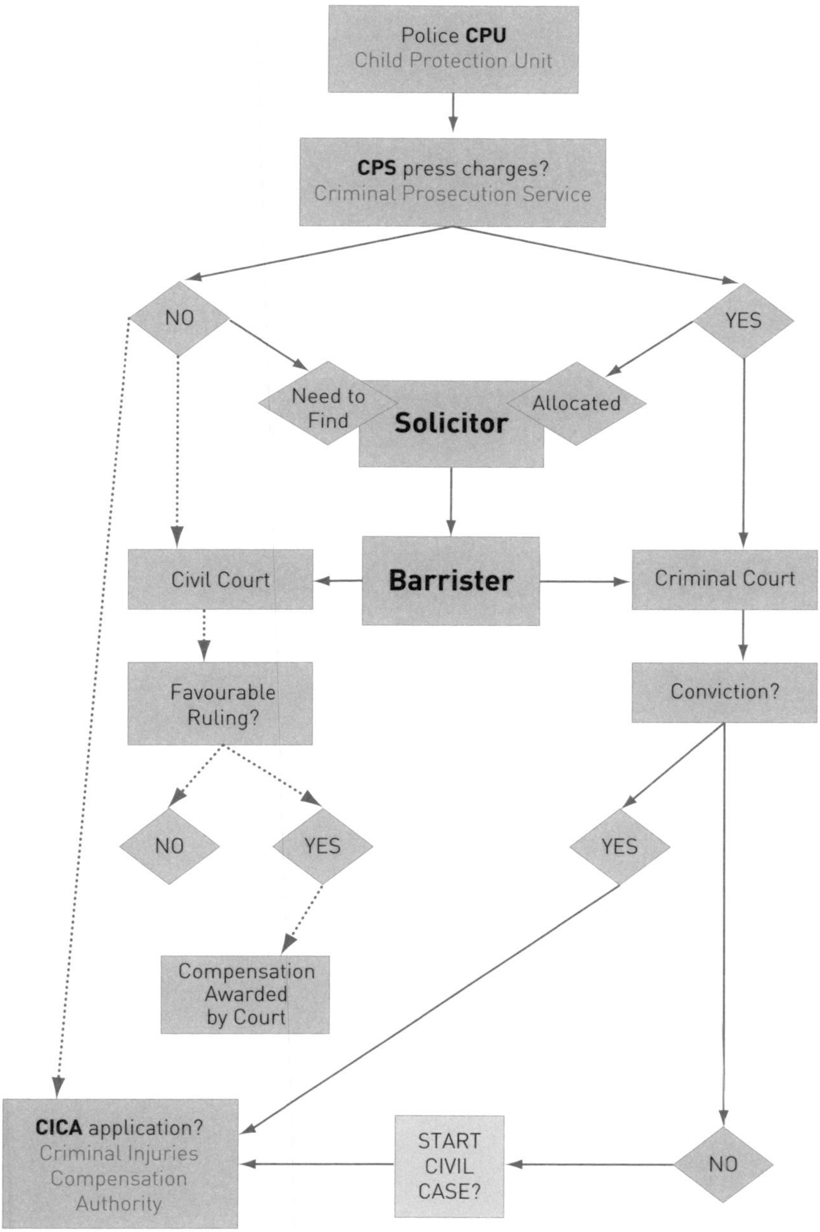

LIFE AFTER COURT

FACING FEELINGS

The end of your legal journey can stir up a lot of feelings and it can be challenging to manage them:

Relief, strength, resolved, ready to move on, proud.
Robbed of childhood, betrayed, enraged, vengeful, untrusting, sad.
Overwhelmed, disappointed, angry or sad, failure, emptiness.
Injustice because the result, sentencing or compensation seems small compared to impact on you.

MAKING THE BEST FROM COMPENSATION

Take the time to know what steps move you in the direction of your dreams. This will help you to invest your financial award in ways that have long lasting rewards for your life. Consider what areas of your life you would like to advance in, being careful to find what makes your heart skip with joy. If you are like me, I have struggled to be clear about what I really want and have needed help to be clearer.

There are specialists such as life coaches and psychologists who provide support to think through and achieve goals; there are also wealth managers or financial advisers who can help with the financial planning. Give yourself time to find second opinions and to thoroughly consider any advise.

Personal experience

I experienced sexual abuse both in my home and in local authority care. I felt disturbed and angry by the council's denial of any wrongdoing especially as my care records and teacher reports were saying something else.

Unfortunately the psychiatric reports were not so supportive, as they related my emotional conditions to other childhood issues; there was also a gap in my medical history due to lost records and an absence of witnesses.

After 4 years of investigation the legal aid was withdrawn due to weak evidence and I had to sign away the right to approach the court again about the issue. While I felt disappointed and betrayed I knew how richer life is from being more true to self.

FOCUS YOUR ENERGY TOWARDS THE BEST FOR YOUR LIFE

As childhood sexual abuse thrives on silence, secrecy and the misuse of power, there is often a stage in recovery that wants to declare the injustice, where the abuser is chastised and there are consequences for harmful actions. This is healthy and understandable.

Whatever legal route you pursue, beware of solely focusing on compensation and/or jail time to help you feel better - there is a lot you can do with the energy from your anger.

You can also use your voice, energy and influence to:

- campaign for change in local, national and/or global services or law,
- support for survivor related services or
- self expression through drama, music, visual art.

SET GOALS

A one degree of change a day will create a full circle of change within a year! Remember, zero will always be zero but one is mother of millions.

There are a number of approaches to being clear about your way forward. Experiment to see what works for you

[A] Go into your imagination to ask

What is it that you really love?
What reality could you create from that?
What obvious actions could be made?
What impact would that create for myself and others?
The to do list may not be easy but it has joy!

[B] Think about your health, finances and relationships

1. Imagine everything is just the way you want it.
2. What does it feel, sound, smell, look like?
3. Rank those goals in level of importance as
    A - an absolute must;
    B - would love to do/have it;
    C - its nice but I can live without it.
4. Give each goal a time frame for completion
5. What steps do you need to reach them?

[C] Make smart goals - specific, measurable, attainable, realistic, time measured

SPECIFIC - describe the goal; when do you want to accomplish it by and the action(s) you will take to accomplish it e.g. I want to sell 10 of my photographs; study at university by year (), set up a successful restaurant within a year and I will find investors and reliable staff.

MEASURABLE - how will you know when you have achieved this goal? Do you check your progress by setting a time, money or by producing something?

ATTAINABLE - Have you got the resources to achieve this goal with your situation and skill level? Is achieving this goal realistic with effort and commitment? Remember to set high goals, but be realistic.

REALISTIC - Why is this goal significant to your work life and/or personal life? Do these goals help you to be more of who you really are? What really motivates you about this goal?

TIME - Goals must have definite starting points and ending points and milestones along the way. We would simply be motivated to put the goal off for a later time and never get around to it.

[D] Weigh up the pros and cons of your goals

Completion Date
Challenges + hindrances
Strategy for facing challenge
Pro's from success
Con's from not attaining

COUNT YOUR ACHIEVEMENTS!

Seeing what you HAVE done more than what you haven't gives you energy! It may feel strange to congratulate yourself for small things because its unfamiliar but the truth is that every small step contributes towards where you want to be!

At the end of each day, you could:

- write a list of what you've achieved today
- tick off your 'To Do' list
- Remember things that you are grateful for, the small and the large things and call it your list or book of treasures!

PRAISE YOUR PERSONAL STRENGTH!

It takes immense honesty, courage, perseverance and great strength to name and face what happened to you! These qualities ccontribute to building trust in yourself and with others. Remind yourself of this!

GIVE POSITIVES!

You have a choice of how you speak and treat yourself, either with positive regards or negative attitude. Choosing to speak positively about yourself will help to increase self-worth so be generous and share words of acknowledgement, thoughtfulness and appreciation.

Create poetic moments - appreciate nature when your senses are pleasantly stimulated by looking, smelling, touching, seeing, hearing the sky, sea, earth and all that moves within it.

(Even the things you need to change are valuable as they give you opportunity to be constructive and creative so there is no need to allow yourself or others to put you down! Quiet the inner critic, applaud the appreciator.)

Making choices about the way you spend your time and energy is crucial for creating a happier, fulfilling life for yourself.

VERY ENCOURAGING PEOPLE - VEP

WHY WE NEED VEP'S?

Healthy human development involves giving care and attention to children's emotional and physical needs. Abusive behaviour ignores these needs, using secrets and trickery to cause pain and fear instead.

For many, recovery will involve building the confidence to experience, identify and express feelings and learning to assert natural human need. Your very encouraging people (VEP's) will help you achieve this without judgement.

Strive to thrive in your life! Build a network of people who you regularly have contact with who support and encourage recovery.

WHO ARE VEP'S?

Sometimes VEP's are not who you would ordinarily expect; hearing about the abuse can confuse and distress friends and family so they behave awkwardly and unsupportively. In the future, this can change but in the meantime it is important for you to be taken seriously and feel heard by those who are able to listen.

VEP's could be someone ...

- from your non abusing family eg/ siblings, parents, aunt, uncle
- known to you like a friend or a GP
- unknown to you but a supportive experienced listener such as a helpline worker or counsellor
- Who has similar experience within a support group or forum (see helpful contacts)

My PERSONAL RIGHTS to -

- Life!
- Be me!
- Make choices
- Have likes and wants, needs and boundaries
- Choose beliefs
- Like who I am
- Live the life I want
- Be happy
- Make mistakes
- Forgive self
- Express self
- Protect body
- Have different opinions
- Acknowledge successes
- Forget all of these rights
- Need reminders

Everybody has these rights!

RESOURCES

USEFUL CONTACTS

POLICE

To locate your local station call 0300 123 1212
or click www.met.police.uk/local

SOLICITORS

Association of Child Abuse Lawyers - ACAL
Tel. 0208 390 4701

Association of Personal Injury Lawyers - APIL
www.apil.com
Tel: 0115 958 0585

www.abuselaw.co.uk/
Tel: 0800 7835969

Child Law Advice Line
Legal advice and representation for children and kids.
www.childabuselawyers.com
0845 120 2948

Family Law Bar Association - FLBA
Represents over 2,500 family barristers and promotes family justice
www.flba.org.uk

EMOTIONAL SUPPORT

SURVIVORS UK

Website: www.survivorsuk.org
Email: info@survivorsuk.org
Information & support to men who have been sexually assaulted at any time in their lives, and those who care for them. One-to-one counselling and support groups for male survivors in the London area. Awareness and training for agencies whose client group includes male survivors.
Helpline: 0845 122 1201

RASASC - Rape and Sexual Abuse Support Centre

Website: www.rasasc.org.uk
Helpline open every day of the year taking calls nationally from female and male survivors as well as non-abusing families, partners, friends and other agencies.
Helpline: 0808 802 9999

THE SURVIVORS TRUST

Website: www.thesurvivorstrust.org
A national umbrella agency for over 125 specialist voluntary sector agencies providing a range of counselling, therapeutic and support services working with women, men and children who are victims/ survivors of rape, sexual violence and childhood sexual abuse.
Helpline: 01788 550554

THE CHILD EXPLOITATION & ONLINE PROTECTION CENTRE (CEOP)

Website: www.ceop.gov.uk

Website: www.thinkuknow.co.uk

Part of the UK police force, CEOP is dedicated to protecting children from sexual abuse wherever they may be, working directly with local and international forces. Also work with children and parents to deliver the unique ThinkuKnow educational programme.

Helpline - 0870 000 3344

THE NATIONAL ASSOCIATION FOR PEOPLE ABUSED IN CHILDHOOD (NAPAC)

Website: www.napac.org.uk

Supporting adults who have been abused as children in any way when they want to talk and receive support.

Helpline: 0800 085 3330

VICTIM SUPPORT

Website: www.victimsupport.org.uk

Free and confidential help to victims of crime, witnesses, their family, friends and anyone else affected throughout England and Wales no matter when the crime took place. Also campaigns for change and provides witness support service in criminal courts

Victim Supportline: 0845 30 30 900

RIGHTS OF WOMEN

Website:www.rightsofwomen.org.uk

email: info@row.org.uk

Training, Policy, Publications and Advicelines:-

General and Family Law	020 7251 6577
Criminal Law and Sexual Violence	020 7251 8887
Immigration and Asylum	020 7490 7689

SOCIAL NETWORKING - Facebook Contacts

Everybody is welcome to join as friends or supporters.
To create a safer environment, administrator approval is required

- The Survivors Trust
- **RoSA** (Rape or Sexual Abuse Support Project)
- **CRASAC** (Coventry Rape and Sexual Assault Centre)
- RespondUK Services for adults and children with learning disabilities who are victims of sexual abuse and other trauma.
- Care Leavers UK
- Care Leavers Reunited

SOCIAL NETWORKING - Staying Safe!

There are plenty of places to post information about ourselves and to communicate with others around the world facebook, forums, interest groups, blogs, chatrooms, email, and instant messaging to name just a few. While you can meet like minded people through social networking sites, you may also be exposed to those who have bad intentions, such as hackers, identity thieves, con artists, predators or even people you know who act spitefully.

Protective Precautions

- Never disclose your address, phone number, date of birth, bank account, credit card numbers or any other personal information through social network sites.

- Do not disclose anything about yourself, your friends, or family members that you wouldn't want to be made public. Please remember that once information appears on a website, it can never be completely erased. Even if it's modified or deleted, older versions may exist on others' computers

- Learn how to restrict access to certain people with your privacy settings BEFORE you start to accept people

SUPPORT FOR YOUR GOALS

GRANTS

When you have some clear goals to improve your life and you are living in hardship then The Directory for Social Change publish two books that could help; **The Guide to Grants for Individuals in Need** and **The Guide to Educational Grants**. Your local reference library usually stock one or two copies for you to look at.

MONEY

Money advice websites:

- www.which.co.uk
- www.moneysavingexpert.com
- www.moneysupermarket.com
- www.nationaldebtline.co.uk

COACHING

CBT - Cognitive Behavioural Therapy
www.babcp.com

NLP - Neuro-Linguistic Programming
http://www.anlp.org

BOOKS

Directory And Book Services (DABS)
Website: www.dabsbooks.co.uk/
The specialist book and information service for people who are overcoming childhood abuse, sexual abuse, or domestic violence.

TITLES

The Courage to Heal Workbook For Women and Men Survivors of Child Sexual Abuse
by Laura Davis
In this groundbreaking companion volume to The Courage to Heal, Laura Davis has created an inspiring, innovative, in-depth workbook for all women and men suffering from the effects of childhood sexual abuse.

Surviving Childhood Sexual Abuse - Practical Self-help for Adults Who Were Sexually Abused as Children.
By Carole Ainscough and Karen Toon

I Never Told Anyone - **Writings by Women Survivors of Child Sexual Abuse**

By Ellen Bass, Louise Thornton.

A reissue of the now-classic anthology (with more than 60,000 copies sold) of deeply moving testimonies by survivors of child sexual abuse)

The Courage to Heal -
A Guide for Women Survivors of Child Sexual Abuse

By Ellen Bass, Laura Davis.

An updated and revised edition of the classic best-selling guide (more than 700,000 copies sold) that has inspired millions of women survivors of child sexual abuse and helped them down the road
to recovery.

Be Heroic!
Protect and lead away
from destructive,
harmful behaviour!

BIGGEST THANKS

With your generous encouragement, skill and time this booklet now exists in a tangible form. May all your dreams come to fruition too.

Marianne Caitane and **Rosalyn Reid** for saying 'Go For It' right from the start!,
Roy Lane and **Emily Miles** - who nurture my voice and truth,
Frederica Lacey - for sharing generosity and wisdom at the crucial moment,
Joan Armatrading for her musicianship and poetry – a guide through dark moods while I lived in care,
Tim Holmes - for artistry and perseverance,
Vida Adamoli's everlasting hugs and affirmations,
Miles Millward for honesty and passion for justice,
Gez Millward for always believing and loving,
Cecilia Joseph and **DS Jason Morgan** for humanising the police process,
Victim Support (Lambeth, UK) - who helped me keep sane through the legal proceedings.

SPECIAL THANKS

Dr Daisaku Ikeda, Honorary President of Soka Gakkai International,
Mrs Kaneko Ikeda,
& Members of SGI-UK particularly in South East London Area, who constantly inspire me through their life examples to win over adversity and support others to do the same.